God's Promise to Abraham, Moses and You

Kingdom Principles for Living Victoriously

John 6:40 — *"And this is the will of Him who sent Me, that everyone who sees the Son and believes in Him may have everlasting life..."*

Book 1

Nancy Williams

Way of Life Publishing

Nancy Williams
Copyright © 2009 by Nancy Williams
Revised 2016, 2023

No part of this book may be reproduced or transmitted in any form or by any means, electronic or mechanical, including photocopying and recording, or by any information storage or retrieval system except as may be expressly permitted in writing by the author. Permission requests are to be addressed in writing at AWayofLifeMinistries.com. All scripture quotations, unless otherwise indicated, are from the New King James Version.

ISBN: **979-8-9875825-0-3**

PRINTED IN THE UNITED STATES OF AMERICA

To order additional copies of this resource,

Visit: AWayofLifeMinistries.com, Barnes and Noble & Amazon.com

E-book available

DEDICATION

To those who read this:

> This is dedicated to you, in the hopes that through this book you will find a deeper meaning in your walk with Christ. I hope a living Christianity will be yours — that you feel how much you are loved; that you see more clearly how the Bible applies to you, and that you will then embrace and incorporate these principles into your way of being and living.

I want to thank and acknowledge my loving husband, Jaycee, and daughter, Natalie, for lovingly and graciously supporting me as I took time away to complete this labor of love.

PREMISE FOR THIS WORK

Based on Romans 3:23 where God says that all have sinned and fall short of the glory of God, it is this book's premise that all of us require healing. We believe it is through sin, starting with Adam and Eve and passed down from generation to generation, that dysfunctional patterns began. It is sin that separates us from God, says Isaiah 59:2.

It is our goal to facilitate:

    1st — Looking at ourselves honestly

    2nd—Accepting God's grace, love, and truth so that

    3rd —We can be set free from our sins

We propose to do this by using God's Word and following His way.

We believe the fruit of this will be:

- An intimate relationship with God the Father, God the Son, and God the Holy Spirit

- The abundant life from God will be ours as we live and grow in this dynamic relationship

- Manifestation of the gifts of the Spirit in us which is for the profit of all, and that God gives as He sees fit and when He sees fit (1 Corinthians 12:7-11). These gifts of the spirit include:

    a. Word of wisdom

    b. Word of knowledge

c. Faith
   d. Gift of healing
   e. Working of miracles
   f. Gift of prophecy
   g. Discerning of spirits
   h. Gift of tongues
   i. Interpretation of tongues

HOW TO USE THESE CHAPTERS

Bringing sinful patterns to the surface and dealing with them according to God's principles will restore your path in life and repair the breach separating you from others and from God, as stated in Isaiah 58:12. Individuals who have gone through this book have found the Holy Spirit and stated that they were empowered and enabled to trust God and look honestly at their lives.

God calls you to live a principled life. As you incorporate His principles in this book, the Holy Spirit will naturally flow through you to others. This book will cover 3 of God's principles as well as a growth plan and emphasizes God's principles, as found in the Bible, as the only source of living victoriously. As God created the world and set up universal principles by which it operates, relational principles are found within this creation and the Bible. He and His principles are the source of life and as you incorporate them, your life will flow smoother with less turmoil and more success. Therefore, memorize some of the given scriptures and the Holy Spirit will bring them to your remembrance in your time of need. "God's Word will not return void" (Isaiah 55:11). You will be affected by memorizing His Word even if you do not feel that an impact is being made. In each chapter, answer the questions to the best of your ability and you will be amazed at what starts happening within you!

This work is divided into 4 books which can be completed separately or sequentially by yourself or within a group setting.

If going through A Way of Life in a group setting, the facilitator may decide to share a short weekly teaching which provides the biblical foundation for the principle/s being reviewed, such as confession or repentance. The main group could then be divided into groups with a group facilitator present to promote sharing what God is doing in each other's lives, what the chapter review has brought to light and any hindrance in depending on God. The main facilitator may bring the whole group back together at the end for sharing and prayer or each group could end their time with prayer. Additional supportive subjects are found in the appendix at the back of each book in this series of 4.

And now, let us continue with discovering and applying

God's Kingdom Principles for Living Victoriously!

INTRODUCTION

Book 1 will explore why and what God's promise is and how to speak to & approach God, our Father. In Book 1, you will learn about Godly submission and that God has His best for you. Being submissive will allow you to learn and believe in how much God loves you, what names He uses for you, and how He sees you.

You may be asking yourself, "What is this promise?" This promise is a covenant that can be defined as a promise between two or more parties to perform certain actions. In the covenant that will be covered in Chapter 1, there are two covenant parties. The first party is God Himself. The second party is you. God promises to always keep his part of the covenant regardless of whether you keep yours, because of WHO He is.

Knowing God's covenant towards you is imperative in your being able to trust Him with your life. If trust is unable to be built, there's no relationship, which God wants with you. That's why it's important for you to know that because of how much God loves you, He created this covenant just for you. More on the covenant in the first chapter.

First, why would He create and make a covenant with you? You might be thinking, "I'm nothing and no one thinks of me as much, so why would God?" The answer is that You are created in the image of God and hence, are very valuable and precious in His sight and loved unconditionally. You are worthy because He says so and He wants a relationship with you. You also have a purpose that you were born to fulfill and as you draw close to God and His way, you will become aware of and can then learn to live out what was ordained for you from the beginning of time.

The Westminster Catechism states, in question 1 with the answer:

- "Q. 1. What is the chief end of man?
- Man's chief end is to glorify God, and to enjoy him forever. 1 Cor. 10:31; Rom. 11:36; Ps. 73:25-28."

So, your goal is to get to know God and enjoy Him and as you do that (and in spite of), He enjoys you as well!

Before beginning, it's important to evaluate how you show up in life and look at how Jesus showed up, as He is our example to follow. You might be wondering, "What is meant by how you show up?" In relationships with others, this means, are your moods and spirit happy, anxious, sad, overbearing, funny, serious, demanding, irritating, or goofy, to name a few. It's what you dole or give out to others and their experience of you. Jesus showed up with tough yet unconditional love for others and knew their heart motives and feelings. The way He showed up was compassionate and He listened well. Jesus could tell when some of the religious leaders were trying to trick Him and called them out about it. His heart was for them to understand the will of His Father and for them to hear Him, but the religious rulers did not. Those that did, allowed Him to change them from the inside out as they got revelation or understanding about what love truly is and how God calls us to act, or *be, from the inside out.*

WHAT DOES IT MEAN TO BE?

You might have heard well-meaning messages about loving one another and treating each other with compassion and kindness while doing what's right. And yet, this message misses the mark. You might attempt to *put on* these character traits rather than *be* them on the inside and then wonder why the results are not evident. Loving, authentic Christianity is not the witness. So why is this? God created you to *be* love and when you are not, there's no authenticity nor behaving from the core of who you were created to be.

Here's your example:

1. Jesus was and is love
2. Jesus loved

Jesus came from an unconditional, divine state of being so He could then love in human flesh. Then, and only then, could He manifest in power, effect, and results. He chose to *be* love and is love. The difference is becoming love (noun) on the inside instead of attempting to put it on and act loving on the outside when we aren't that on the inside. We attempt to be what we are not which is what Jesus came to change. Transformation is the process and freedom is the result. Free to be who we were created to be!

So, like Jesus, you are to live and *be*, powered by the choice to love and be love. Being love is by choice, intention, and commitment, empowered by His Holy Spirit. When you choose love and allow the Holy Spirit to guide you, you are your authentic self.

Remember, others live with you and more importantly, you live with yourself. The million-dollar question is, "How do you want to live with yourself?" Would you want to be the type of person who is open, calm, joyful, authentic, honest, and loving or the opposite? If you want the former, you get to choose to follow the example Jesus gave us of unconditional, authentic love. Then abundant life can flow through you to others and this life can be true, pure, and lovely. When you **are** unconditional love, you are truly free.

> Free to fly to the music of His joy,
> Free to feel the waves tumble us in playfulness,
> Free Choice—
> The way it is meant to be.

THE HOLY SPIRIT

In this world, the war against good and evil is extremely evident. On one side is the good side, with peace and harmony. The other side is dark, which is evil. There is a call on the dark side to all who will hear to succumb to the pull of power, anger, death and destruction. This evil pull is so strong that it separates families, friends, and even those in power.

God, in the person of the Holy Spirit, is a counselor and giver of knowledge and wisdom. God, in the person of the Holy Spirit, will come into your heart to be your guide and strength if you ask Him to! How this works will be covered throughout the rest of this book.

There are good and evil forces at work around you—ALL the time. You may or may not be aware of the evil temptations that pull you to do wrong things. To become a warrior of God, this work will support you in becoming more aware as well as increasing your connection with the Holy Spirit. You will learn how the Holy Spirit can guide you into all truth, and warn you of danger, to list a few of the works He does!

As an example of how the Holy Spirit may talk to you, I will share an experience I had where the Holy Spirit gave me a gift of knowledge. At a church I was attending, I was on the prayer team. A lady wanted prayer and as I interviewed her, she told me why she needed prayer. While I prayed for what she wanted, the Holy Spirit, and a still small voice inside of me, kept impressing me to ask about her boyfriend. In obedience, I asked her about her boyfriend, and she was SHOCKED! "How did you know?" she asked. I said that God revealed this to me (a nagging impression) because He loved her and so she could be set free. That night, she was when we prayed for her real need.

God works to free His people and the workers are few. That is why this book was written. This book is for you, who are open to the light, want to live victoriously and tell others the good news.

Contents

DEDICATION	iii
PREMISE FOR THIS WORK	iv
HOW TO USE THESE CHAPTERS	vi
INTRODUCTION	viii
CHAPTER 1 THE COVENANT, SIN, GRACE & MERCY	1
CHAPTER 2 SURRENDER & ACCEPTANCE	29
CHAPTER 3 SALVATION & LETTING GO OF CONTROL	43
CHAPTER 4 SANCTIFICATION: PERSONAL GROWTH PLAN FOR ASSIMILATION & PRINCIPLE PRACTICE	58
CONCLUSION	63
SUGGESTED READING LIST	64
APPENDIX TABLE OF CONTENTS	67
USING A WAY OF LIFE IN A GROUP SETTING	68
DEPENDENCE ON GOD	70
DAILY ACCEPTANCE PRAYER	72
THE FIRST AND SECOND GREATEST COMMANDMENTS	73
THE TEN COMMANDMENTS	75
THE WAY IT IS MEANT TO BE	77
GOAL SETTING	79
BIBLIOGRAPHY	85
ABOUT THE AUTHOR	90

As each part of A Way of Life can be purchased separately, some of the same writings are duplicated in some or each part of this book series. Examples include the growth plan and, in the appendix, goal setting.

CHAPTER 1

THE COVENANT, SIN, GRACE & MERCY

A covenant relationship with God and how you understand this relationship is vital to receiving the Holy Spirit from God and trusting Him. Read the following while allowing the Holy Spirit to touch and speak to you.

In the beginning, God created the heavens and the earth and all that was in them. He created Adam and Eve and talked and walked with them in a special, holy, and right relationship. They were given the command to take care of the earth and have dominion over it. Everything lived in harmony as there was a perfect union between God, man, and the world He had made.

In the Garden of Eden, Satan, whose original name was Lucifer and who had been a powerful angel in heaven, had previously been thrown from heaven as he wanted power and be above God. A third of the angels sided with him and were thrown to the earth with him. Satan's goal then, and now, is to keep as many people as possible away from God and going towards a path of death and destruction. Therefore, in the Garden of Eden, Satan tempted Adam and Eve to doubt God and choose their way rather than God's way, which they did (the sin of disobedience).

When they chose to do the one thing God asked them not to do (eat of one tree's fruit), disobedience and sin entered the world, and man fell from having a right relationship with God and from having dominion over the earth. The decay started in the human and earthly realms, and there was division and disharmony, which has been passed down from generation to generation.

But God had a plan to rectify this travesty. God sent His only son, Jesus, to restore His and our relationship to the way it was intended to be, in Genesis. Jesus restored this relationship by shedding His blood on the cross to pay for our disobedience to His ways and to break the bondage of sin over us. God then, looks at all who believe that Jesus died for their sins on the cross, as flawless. As white as snow. As perfect and complete without blemish. But why Jesus, you might ask? Before Jesus' death, the people of God shed blood for the forgiveness of their sins by shedding an unblemished animal's blood through animal sacrifice.

Jesus came so that we do not have to pay the price of spiritual death (eternal separation from God) for our sins nor shed animal blood. He, who is unblemished, shed His blood for us and rose from the dead so that we may live. He opened the way to God through His death and resurrection, saying, "I am the way, the truth, and the life. No one comes to the Father except through Me" (John 14:6). Because of God's mercy, we who believe in Jesus' death and resurrection have been forgiven and will not receive the judgment due us. Jesus conquered Satan, the power of death, the power of our flesh and the power of sin over us with His death and resurrection. In Him, we are victors. Satan, our flesh and sin have no power over us that we do not allow.

Ephesians 6 lists the protective armor God provides for every Christian, which includes the helmet of salvation, breastplate of righteousness, belt of truth, feet shod with the gospel of peace, sword of the spirit, and shield of faith. I encourage you to study this to learn how to fight the good fight of faith!

Webster's Dictionary defines a covenant as "a formal, solemn, and binding agreement." The Bible tells us in Genesis 1:12-15 that God made such a covenant with Abraham that the world would be blessed through him and his descendants. The Bible, God's Word, is divided into the Old and New Testaments, which correspond to the Old and New Covenants.

The Old Covenant (Old Testament) was a promise from God to those who left Egypt and were being led by Him to the Promised Land. To Moses (descendent of Abraham) and the children of Israel, God said in Exodus 19:5-6, "If you will indeed obey My voice and keep My covenant, then you shall be a special treasure to Me above all people; for all the earth is Mine. And you shall be to Me a kingdom of priests and a holy nation." T.B. Maston, in his book Biblical Ethics, states, "God is always the initiator of the covenant; it is not a contract between two people of equal or near-equal standing. It is unilateral. GOD ALONE states the conditions of the covenant; the people could not negotiate with God regarding the covenant nor change its conditions. They could either accept or reject it. Once accepted, they could not annul it but could violate its conditions. God alone had the power to dissolve the covenant, which He never used. God is revealed not only as a covenant-giving but also as a covenant-keeping God."

The Ten Commandments, given by God, were then given to Moses for the people of God in Exodus 20 as their part of the covenant relationship. As God promises to lead, guide, and protect His people, He also requires His people to obey His Word. Israel accepted the covenant to do as God commanded verbally in Exodus 19 and ratified by a blood sacrifice in Exodus 24, after the specific behavior obligations for God's people (the Ten Commandments) were laid down in stone.

Circumcision was given as a sign for every male child to show that God would be their God. They became a set-apart people, a peculiar people into the beginnings of a community of true worshipers of God. God gave the land of Canaan to Abraham, Isaac, and then Jacob (Genesis 35:12). He permitted no man to do them wrong as they went from one nation to another, saying, "Do not touch My anointed ones, and do My prophets no harm" (1 Chronicles 16:22). God was promising to protect and guide this special community. Abraham "believed God and it was accounted to him for righteousness", which is why he is called the father of the faithful (Galatians 3:6-7). Likewise, God calls us to believe Him and be His people.

Throughout the exodus from Egypt, God directed His people by a pillar of cloud by day and a pillar of fire by night and provided for their thirst, hunger, and protection (Exodus 13-17). Similarly, God desires to guide and provide for His people today. The Old Testament continually pointed to the coming Messiah, the King of kings and Lord of lords. Jesus, in the New Covenant, came to fulfill what had been proclaimed. Again, God had a plan which was and is to continue to gather a people to Himself.

Jesus came as the New Covenant, to write His Word not on stone, as in the Old Covenant, but on the tablets of our hearts (2 Corinthians 3:3). As we receive and accept the work that Jesus did on the cross for us, He gives us Himself in the Person of the Holy Spirit to "teach you all things" (John 14:26) as well as "guide you into all truth; for He will not speak on His own authority, but whatever He hears He will speak; and He will tell you things to come" (John 16:13). This Holy Spirit is given to indwell us, to lead and guide us, if we accept the fact that Jesus paid the penalty of our sins by dying on the cross as a living sacrifice.

So, Jesus won the battle over Satan through His death and resurrection and has given us all the tools necessary to make disciples of all nations (Matthew 28:19). The battle armor of Ephesians 6, previously listed, helps us take back the land that has been usurped by Satan, the world and our flesh. We can do it because Jesus said, "Lo, I am with you always, even to the end of the age" (Matthew 28:20).

Are we sons of Abraham who believe what God says? AS WE BELIEVE GOD AND WHAT HE SAYS, THIS IS THE KEY TO THE KINGDOM BEING ESTABLISHED HERE ON EARTH AS IT IS IN HEAVEN. Satan does not want this to happen! When we pray to receive Christ as our savior, God gives us a permanent, covenantal relationship. This covenant is a sacred, holy, reverent bond and Satan hates it.

What does our side of the covenant consist of? Jesus sacrificed Himself in obedience to God, the Father. Have we sacrificed ourselves in obedience to God's Word? Romans 12:1 calls us to be a "living sacrifice" — to die to self, I, and me, which is contrary to our American society. When we live for ourselves, we try to meet our needs through control, manipulation and guilt, which quench love and keep us in bondage. We were made in the image of God and God is love. To live in freedom, we get to die to ourselves so that God's love can reign in us. Where are we in our decision for God? Have we entered into a relationship with Jesus by accepting Him only and by making a sacrifice of our will to His will? Jesus promises, "He who loses his life for My sake will find it" (Matthew 10:39).

There are conditions to God's many promises that we are responsible to fulfill. Do we ask for the promises but forget about the conditions? For instance, God promises us in James 4:7 that the devil will flee from us. The conditions stated are that we are to submit ourselves to God and resist the devil — then and only then does the promise come that the devil will flee from us. Romans 8:28 states that "all things work together for good to those who love God, to those who are the called according to His purpose," which is fellowship with Him and obedience to His commands. A non-believer cannot stand on this promise of God, ".... that all things work together for good" as they don't have fellowship with Him. As we cease rebelling and follow the conditions stated in God's Word, our lives become peaceful and more harmonious. It is the way we are meant to live. God knows what works and what doesn't. He created it all!

If we want Him to speak to us, we can come to Him as little children in simple faith, seeking His will to be worked in our lives. God promises that if you "Ask it will be given to you; seek, and you will find; knock, and it will be opened to you". Matthew 7:7). How God speaks to us will be covered in another section but know that if we sincerely want to hear from Him, we will!

God has always been there to direct our lives and always will be. Look at Acts, chapter 13 where Barnabas and Saul were sent out to a particular region through the direction of the Holy Spirit (yes, God can impress upon us, what we are to do). This same Spirit is available to lead us into all truth and to show us things to come (John 16:13). As we seek God's way and not our own, clarity will come to our mind and heart regarding the direction we are to go.

The Holy Spirit is the Third Person of our Triune God (Trinity). He has distinctive characteristics of personality: knowledge (1 Corinthians 2:10-11), will (1 Corinthians 12:11), mind (Romans 8:27), love (Romans 15:30), goodness (Nehemiah 9:20) and grief (Ephesians 4:30). R.A. Torrey portrays that The Holy Spirit is not a blind, impersonal influence or power that comes into our lives to illuminate, sanctify, and empower us. He is a holy Person who comes to dwell in our hearts. One who knows fully every act we perform, every word we speak, every thought we entertain that is allowed to pass through our minds. If there is anything in thought, word, or action that is impure, unholy, unkind, selfish, mean, petty, or untrue, this infinitely Holy One is deeply grieved by it.

What is our relationship with this Holy One? It has been my experience that as I have sincerely asked my Father to reveal His truth to me and the path, He has ordained for me, He does so through the Person of the Holy Spirit. He promises to! I can rest and wait for His Word to me. This Holy Spirit, the third Person of the Trinity, penetrates and guides us into living out the abundant life God has created and ordained for each of us.

Do you see that God is calling a special people to Himself — a holy people — a holy nation? Do you see that God has won the battle? Satan has been defeated and God has always had a plan to draw His creation unto Himself. He promises always to be there for you to guide and protect, for only that which He allows can touch you. He has given you His own Spirit with which to go forth and make disciples of all nations and if you are God's, you are a force to be reckoned with—a Warrior of God!

I have shown the continual promise of God to a people (you) who set themselves apart for Him and Him alone. Can you accept and believe? Can you appreciate all that God gave you at the death and resurrection of Jesus? I hope that A Way of Life will help you understand what He has given you. I hope you will draw closer to God and receive the abundant life He offers you.

THE LAW

The law can be defined as that which proceeds from the mouth of God (God's Word) to outline the way you are to live. There are several categories of God's law, and one category is the Law of Moses, which includes the Ten Commandments. The primary purpose of the law is to convict you of your sin and help restrain wickedness. It exists so that you can realize that you will never be perfect and cannot save yourself. The law points out the need for some other means or method of freedom from the inherent guilt that stems from your inability to keep God's law, which is why Jesus came. He paid the price due you and took your guilt with Him, to the cross.

SIN

The Greek word translated as "sin" (hamartia) means "missing the mark." It is an archer's term, picturing an arrow that flies toward the target but falls short. Sin is defined as anything contrary to the law of God, for 1 John 3:4 declares, "sin is lawlessness." Scripture tells us that sin is against God and our neighbor. Just as there is an absolute with good, so is there an absolute with sin. It is either sin or not sin. Sin stems from the heart, so does not consist of outward habits or acts alone. Sinful heart attitudes, thoughts and intentions can lead to sinful deeds. The result is true guilt before our Maker, making you liable for punishment, and causing death within you (Romans 6:23).

GRACE

By the law of God, you know sin. By sin, you are guilty. Grace then, is the unearned love of God toward you. The Greek word most often translated as "grace" in the New Testament (Charis) is defined as favor, acceptance, kindness granted, and favor done *without expectation of return*. It is a gift of the loving-kindness of God to you. It is a completely *unearned and unmerited favor*. The Holy Spirit enables you to walk God's way of life with favor and is one of His greatest graces.

For God's grace to provide healing from our sins, you must first genuinely want help. You must recognize that something is missing in your life. In society, you were likely taught to be competitive, proud of your accomplishments, look good, and not let others control you. This outward appearance is what you likely used to give yourself worth as an individual. You may not be in touch with who you are on the inside and may be covered in denial. This makes you lonely and unable to connect with others. You can find yourself when you relinquish control to the Almighty, who made you. You who think you're in control are not. It is only when you trust your creator that you are set free to be who you were created to be.

MERCY

Grace and mercy are closely related. God's mercy means that He will not put on you the judgment or consequences of your sin that you deserve. The misery of sin will be removed by God's mercy if the guilt and power of sin are removed through God's grace first. You, in turn, can be merciful to others as God has been merciful to you.

The following questions are designed to explore your perceptions, thought processes and behaviors — all to support your growth into freedom and support the awakening of the Holy Spirit within you.

As you look at life, your understanding of God's law is:

Your understanding of sin is:

The Holy Spirit throughout your life will bring different sins to your attention for the purpose of:

- Collaborating with you to rid yourself of them
- Being in a closer relationship with your Heavenly Father

Many times, however, you won't want to work with the Holy Spirit as you then get to look at yourself.

The ways in which you have denied looking at yourself include:

A Way Of Life

The outstanding sin or sins in your life right now are:

When you hear of God's grace, you understand this to be:

What message have you received from society or your parents relating to your worth as a person? What is/or was important to them regarding the way others looked at them or your family?

What area of your life has been the most unmanageable?

How have you tried to manage your life in the past?

What behaviors do you find yourself employing to manage your life?

A Way Of Life

What have been the consequences of those behaviors?

Why shouldn't you depend on yourself for your life? (Romans 7:18, *"I know that in me [this is, in my flesh] nothing good dwells; for to will is present with me, but how to perform what is good I do not find."*)

In what way does God say that you are powerless, in Romans 7:15? *"For what I am doing, I do not understand. For what I will to do, that I do not practice; but what I hate, that I do."*

What fears about examining your true self do you have?

What does God say about the peace that He gives to you, in John 14:27? *"Peace I leave with you, My peace I give to you; not as the world gives do I give to you. Let not your heart be troubled, neither let it be afraid."*

What is your belief about God's covenant relationship with you?

A Way Of Life

What doubts do you have that He made this covenant with you?

What did the shedding of Jesus' blood on the cross do for you?

In your heart of hearts, do you believe it is enough to cover all?

Nancy Williams

What does Jesus' blood not cover for you?

A LOOK AT MY FAMILY

Let's be honest. All families are dysfunctional due to the fall of Adam and Eve, so no one is exempt in this area. The difference is how dysfunctional a family unit is. It seems to me that the farther we stray from God's Kingdom Principles being lived out in the family unit, the more dysfunction is present in the family. I have included the following exercise to discover the truth about your family of origin, so you can be healed. As you learn the Kingdom Principles of Living Victoriously, you can bring your needs to God and others to ask for healing. Use the following list to identify where you need healing. The list and definitions below are taken from The Family by John Bradshaw (Health Communications, Inc. 1988), and are used with permission from the author.

Directions: Read each definition. If the definition pertains to you, come back to this page, and circle the letter below. Continue to the next letter and the corresponding definition. Repeat until you have read all the letters and definitions for Adult Children of Dysfunctional Families.

A	Abandonment Issues
D	Delusion and Denial
U	Undifferentiated Ego Mass
L	Loneliness and Isolation
T	Thought Disorders
C	Control Madness
H	Hyper-vigilant and High-Level Anxiety
I	Internalized Shame
L	Lack of Boundaries

D	Disabled Will
R	Reactive and Re-enacting
E	Equifinality
N	Numbed Out
O	Offender with or without Offender Status
F	Fixated Personality
D	Dissociated Responses
Y	Yearning for Parental Warmth and Approval
S	Secrets
F	Faulty Communication Style
U	Under-involved
N	Neglect of Developmental Dependency Needs
C	Compulsive/Addictive
T	Trance
I	Intimacy Problems
O	Over-involved
N	Narcissistically Deprived
A	Abuse Victim
L	Lack of Coping Skills (under-learning)

F	False Self—confused Identity
A	Avoid Depression through Activity
M	Measured, Judgmental, and Perfectionist
I	Inhibited Trust
L	Loss of Your Own Reality
I	Inveterate Dreamer
E	Emotional Constraint
S	Spiritual Bankruptcy

A. ABANDONMENT ISSUES

One or both of your parents physically abandoned you. Or, they might have been physically present but not emotionally available to you. Someone in your family physically, sexually, or emotionally violated you. Your developmental dependency needs were neglected. You were enmeshed in your parents' neediness or in the needs of your family system. You stay in relationships far beyond what is healthy.

D. DELUSION AND DENIAL

You think you had a great childhood and that your family was the good old American Family.

U. UNDIFFERENTIATED EGO MASS

You carry the feelings, desires and secrets of other people in your family system.

L. LONELINESS AND ISOLATION

You have felt lonely all or most of your life. You feel isolated and different.

T. THOUGHT DISORDERS

You get preoccupied with generalities or details. You worry, ruminate and obsess a lot. You stay in your head to avoid your feelings. You read about your problems rather than act.

C. CONTROL MADNESS

You try to control yourself and everyone else. You feel extremely uncomfortable when you're out of control. You mask your efforts to control people and situations by "being helpful."

H. HYPER-VIGILANT AND HIGH ANXIETY

You live on guard. You are easily startled. You panic easily.

I. INTERNALIZED SHAME

You feel flawed as a human being. You feel inadequate and hide behind a role or an addiction or character trait like control, blame, criticism, perfectionism, contempt, power, and rage.

L. LACK OF BOUNDARIES

You don't know where you end and others begin — physically, emotionally, intellectually, or spiritually. You don't know what you really stand for.

D. DISABLED WILL

You are willful. You try to control other people. You are grandiose. With you, it's all or nothing.

R. REACTIVE AND RE-ENACTING

You react easily. You feel things that are not related to what is happening. You feel things more intensely than the event calls for. You find yourself repeating patterns over and over.

E. EQUIFINALITY

No matter where you begin, your life seems to end at the same place.

N. NUMBED OUT

You don't feel your feelings. You don't know what you feel. You don't know how to express what you feel.

O. OFFENDER WITH OR WITHOUT OFFENDER STATUS

You offend people, or you play that role occasionally.

F. FIXATED PERSONALITY

You are an adult, but your emotional age is very young. You look like an adult but feel very childlike and needy. You feel like a lifeguard on a crowded beach, but you don't know how to swim. (You're in charge but you don't know what to do)

D. DISSOCIATED RESPONSES

You have no memories of painful events of your childhood; you have a split personality; you depersonalize; can't remember people's names, even people you were with only two years ago. You are out of touch with your body and your feelings.

Y. YEARN FOR PARENTAL WARMTH AND APPROVAL – YOU SEEK IT IN OTHER RELATIONSHIPS

You still try to gain your parents' approval. You yearn for the perfect relationship. You have an exaggerated need for others' approval. You fear offending others. You find emotionally unavailable partners (just like your parents were), whom you try to make love you. You will go to almost any lengths to care for and help your partner. Almost nothing is too much trouble. Having had little nurturing yourself, you find people who need nurturing and take care of them.

S. SECRETS

You carry lots of secrets from your family of origin. You've never talked to anyone about how bad it was in your family, and you carry lots of secrets about your own life. You also carry lots of sexual secrets you would not want to tell anyone.

F. FAULTY COMMUNICATION

You have had trouble communicating in every relationship you've been in. No one seems to understand what you say. You feel confused when communicating with others. When talking to your parents, no matter how good your intentions are to be sane and clear, the results are conflicting and confusing.

U. UNDER-INVOLVED

You stand on the sidelines of life, wishing you were a participant. You don't know how to initiate a relationship, a conversation, or an activity. You are withdrawn and would rather bear the pangs of being alone than risk interaction. You are not spontaneous. You allow yourself very little excitement or fun.

N. NEGLECT OF DEVELOPMENTAL DEPENDENCY NEEDS

You have a hole in the cup of your psyche. You never seem to be satisfied. No matter how much you anticipate something, soon after it is over, you feel restless and unsatisfied. You are childish and feel like a child most of the time. You cry when someone says beautiful things about you. You feel like you don't really belong wherever you are.

C. COMPULSIVE/ADDICTIVE

You have been or are now in an active compulsive addictive behavior.

T. TRANCE

You are fantasy bonded and still idealize your parents, continuing to play the role you played in your family system. Nothing has really changed in your family of origin: the same dialogue, the same fights and the same gossip. Your marriage or your relationship is like that of your parents.

I. INTIMACY PROBLEMS

You have trouble in relationships. You have been married more than twice, choosing partners who embody the same emotional patterns as your primary caretakers. You are attracted to seductive, psychopathic partners; you are not attracted to partners who are kind, stable, reliable, and interested in you. You find nice men and women boring. When you start getting too close, you leave a relationship. You confuse closeness with compliance, intimacy with fusion.

O. OVER-INVOLVED

You are drawn to people who are needy. You confuse love with pity. You are drawn to people who have problems you can get involved in fixing. You are drawn toward people and situations that are chaotic, uncertain, and emotionally painful.

N. NARCISSISTICALLY DEPRIVED

You feel empty and childishly helpless inside. You compensate with addiction to such things as chemicals, food, prestige, money, possessions, heroism, sex, power, or violence as a way of feeling important and worthwhile.

A. ABUSE VICTIM

You were physically, emotionally, or sexually abused as a child. You have become a victim in life and play that role in all areas of your life. You feel hopeless about changing anything. Or, you were abused and have become an offender. You identified with the abusive parent or caretaker and act just like he or she did.

L. LACK OF COPING SKILLS (UNDER-LEARNING)

You never learned how to do many things necessary for a fully functional life. Your methods of problem-solving do not work, but you continue to use the same ones over and over. You learned ways of caring for your wounds that, in fact, perpetuated them. You have no real knowledge of what is normal. Your bottom-line tolerance is quite abnormal.

F. FALSE SELF – CONFUSED IDENTITY

Your self-worth depends on your partner's success or failure. When you're not in a relationship, you feel an inner void. You feel responsible for making your partner happy. You take care of people to give yourself an identity. You wear masks, calculate, manipulate, and play games. You act out rigid family or sex roles. When your partner has a stomachache, you take Pepto-Bismol!

A. AVOID DEPRESSION THROUGH ACTIVITY

You get involved in unstable relationships. The more you are physically and mentally active, the more you can avoid depression.

M. MEASURED, JUDGMENTAL, AND PERFECTIONIST

You have unrealistic expectations of yourself and others. You are rigid and inflexible, overly judgmental of yourself and others. You are stuck in your attitudes and behavior, even though it hurts to live the way you do.

I. INHIBITED TRUST

You really don't trust anyone, including your own feelings, perceptions, and judgments.

L. LOSS OF YOUR OWN REALITY — DAMAGED AND WEAK BOUNDARIES

You take more than 50 percent of the responsibility, guilt, and blame for whatever happens in a relationship. You know what others feel or need before you know your own feelings and needs. Rather than take any risk of abandonment, you have withdrawn and refuse to get involved. You regard any change in the status quo of a relationship as a threat. You feel embarrassed by what others do and take inappropriate responsibility for their behavior.

I. INVETERATE DREAMER

You are more in touch with your dreams of how things could be, rather than with the reality of your life and situation. You live according to an ideal image of yourself, having a grandiose and exaggerated notion of yourself. You fantasize, catastrophize and exaggerate the seriousness of decisions and events.

E. EMOTIONAL CONSTRAINT (WITH OR WITHOUT DRAMATIC OUTBURST)

You believe that controlling your emotions is a way to control your life. You attempt to manage your life and your emotions. You have dramatic inappropriate outbursts of emotions that have been repressed for long periods of time. For example, you yell at your children after holding in your anger all day at work. You compulsively expose your emotions. You go to great lengths to verbalize every feeling as soon as it enters your awareness. You do this so that you won't have to feel them for very long.

S. SPIRITUAL BANKRUPTCY

You believe that your worth and happiness lie outside yourself. You have no awareness of your inner life since you spend all your energy avoiding your shame-based inner self.

All the families we have examined so far with items from the prior list have certain structural similarities which are listed here:

- A dominant dysfunction causes a threat to which all other family members respond
- The adaptations to the threat cause the system to close in a frozen and rigid pattern
- The frozen pattern is maintained by each member playing one or more rigid roles
- There is a high level of anxiety and confusion
- Members are shame-based, and shame is the organizing principle of all dysfunctional families
- The more the system tries to change, the more it stays the same

Think about what you just circled and then answer the following questions:

What issues from the list stand out the most for you right now?

A Way Of Life

What do you see differently about your family of origin now than before reading this material?

In what areas of your life do you have trouble setting boundaries?

At what emotional age do you see yourself?

Another reference to support learning of your family of origin and how they handled conflict and love, is the book, How We Love (CO: Alive Communications, 2017) by Milan & Kay Yerkovich. Examples of what they cover are how individuals with a Pleaser love style interact when married with a Vacillator. Or how the Avoider Love style interacts when married to a Pleaser. Other love styles include the Chaotic (Controller and Victim) and Secure Connector. I highly recommend ordering this book and reading it as this work does not include love style information. See their website for a helpful quiz to identify what love style you are operating in and what you can do about your communication style.

> Scripture to memorize this week: Romans 7:15 — *"For what I am doing, I do not understand. For what I will to do, that I do not practice; but what I hate, that I do."*

CHAPTER 2

SURRENDER & ACCEPTANCE

SURRENDER

Hebrews 13:8 teaches that "Jesus Christ is the same yesterday, today, and forever." He came to reconcile you to God and give you His spirit to make you whole. God is in control and if you do not acknowledge this truth, you likely will feel alone, isolated, and defeated. You may feel as if you can take care of yourself and that there is little need for support from other people or God. You may feel as if you are in control, but this is not freedom.

This control, or attempts to control yourself or situations, results in bondage and loneliness. You may feel that there are all these rules that you have to follow to be OK. This control over your actions likely comes from the outside and not the inside which does not permit living in harmony with yourself. Because you can't control your life by yourself, you might be tormented with thoughts of what you should or shouldn't have done. This isn't how God means for you to live. You can't control everything and willingly yield control of your life to Christ.

To surrender, many emotions might come up for you such as:

- Fear —You may experience fear as you confront your past experiences with religion which may not have been positive
- You can start to feel openness
- The ability to experience life and emotions begins—you

- begin to experience your true self
- Humility happens—you become teachable
- False expectations of yourself begin to diminish and the ought to, should and shouldn't no longer control you
- Spontaneity begins to happen

How can you let go of control and surrender?

- God establishes the initial relationship through salvation, but you can deepen that bond through faithful prayer, reading His Word, and getting together with other Christians
- Remember that God is in control but has given you freedom of choice hoping you will follow Him
- Talk to God about everything. Don't be afraid to talk to Him because He already knows what is in your mind and heart
- Listen, seek, and expect answers. God will always answer, but the answer may be "Yes", "No" or "Wait" and it may not come immediately

ACCEPTANCE

You are restored as you accept God's way. As you surrender and accept the fact that through the work of God's Holy Spirit, He will change you to what God intended you to be, do, and then have before He even created you. He has a plan for your life! Many times, you may believe that He wants to benefit and support others but do not believe that for yourself.

He is asking you to begin to trust Him. He is asking you to believe that He loves you and has a plan and purpose for your life. Depending on your background, you may view God as an angry, controlling authority figure with His finger stretched out, condemning you. You may have anger toward Him because He did not do as you asked in a situation nor intervened as you wanted Him to. Maybe you are continuing to want things to go your way? God is asking you to surrender your will to His will for your life. Since He is the I AM and has the universe in the palm of His hand, how much more does He know your needs? You can trust Him.

God is your Creator and the Maker of the heavens and the earth. This doctrine of creation will not be discussed in detail here, but I would like to encourage you to look at nature. Contemplate it. Look at how wonderfully made the human body is. Even with the abuse of high stress, drugs, alcohol, and food, our bodies fight to function harmoniously. The Creator of the universe exists and is the force that holds all things together. As you truly come to recognize the depth and breadth of Him, you will or are compelled to fall at His feet in surrender and acceptance. The Christian paradox is that **man is never completely free** until he **totally submits to God.**

Scripture to memorize: Zechariah 4:6 — "'Not by might nor by power, but by My Spirit,' says the Lord of hosts."

List the thoughts that come to mind as you think of the word Father. Include what your relationship was with your father, as you were growing up:

Depending upon your past experiences, your response to God being your heavenly Father will either be pleasant, unpleasant or a combination of the two. It is important to become aware of your response and to understand the perceptions you hold of Him. Many times, you may see God as you see your own father which is never an accurate picture. As you become aware of the misperceptions you might hold, you can then throw them away and embrace the truth about God.

Your perception of God can determine how readily you will come to Him and begin to trust Him, which will affect His working in your life to free you from the bondage you may be in. As you recognize your sins or misperceptions, tell God about them by going to Him in repentance.

Accept His forgiveness and your responsibility to work with Him in your change and He will set you free. Jesus said, "If you abide in My Word, you are my disciples indeed. And you shall know the truth, and the truth shall make you free" (John 8:31-32).

A Way Of Life

DRAW A PICTURE OF GOD'S FACE WHEN YOU THINK OF HIM LOOKING AT YOU

Terms to describe your view of God (e.g., harsh judge, forgiving, angry, loving):

I cannot look or come to God because:

When I consider that God is my Father, my reaction is:

A Way Of Life

I never had, or lost my faith in God because of the following experiences:

Romans 10:17 says, that "Faith comes by hearing, and hearing by the Word of God." You can exercise your faith by obeying His Word no matter how you feel and lifting your fear/s to Him. As you risk, your trust in Him grows and you can lay more and more of your life down to His care. As you commune more and more with Him, you will begin to identify and experience His operation in your life. Your faith will increase and your sensitivity to His voice will grow.

In what way do you see God operating in your life right now?

We are a people of the "now" generation. We are not usually willing to wait, anticipate, or work through anything in our lives. Just know that implementing God's principles in your life is not usually an immediate occurrence so frustration may be a temptation. Realize that spiritual growth and healing are individual, so do not be discouraged if you do not feel that you are moving as fast as you want to.

The above being said, you can grow with God as fast as you want. It depends on your desire and commitment to pursue Him and learn of yourself. See the dependence circle on page 70. As you learn of yourself, take what you've learned back to Him in prayer, and ask Him to change you. Ask what actions you get to take to support the change and then apply what you hear. You will be amazed at how fast you will change!

What is your reaction to the time it takes for spiritual growth and healing?

In what areas do you see God restoring you to His original intention?

A Way Of Life

What does God say about fear and your mind, in 2 Timothy 1:7— *"God has not given us a spirit of fear, but of power, and of love and of a sound mind."*

Allow this scripture to affect your emotions. How does it feel?

What does God say about times of trouble in Psalm 40:1-2, *"I waited patiently for the Lord; and He inclined to me and heard my cry. He also brought me up out of a horrible pit, out of the miry clay, and set my feet upon a rock, and established my steps."*

List any areas where you are having doubt in believing that God is your Father, that He wants the best for you and has the power to save you and lift you up into the abundant life— see John 10:10.

God uses other individuals who have gone through similar experiences to help you see your own life clearer and to obtain some direction. He calls all of us to be a spiritual family who bears one another's burdens (Galatians 6:2).

What experiences have you had in the past of sharing yourself with others—either among your family of origin, friends, or church family?

A Way Of Life

How does being involved with others fulfill your need for a spiritual family?

The following exercise will also support the identification of what your perception is regarding your family of origin. The adaptability and attachment scales may bring to light ways of relating that have been passed down from generation to generation. There are no right answers or perfect families, so please be truthful with yourself!

FAMILY INVENTORY

From Forgiving Our Parents, Forgiving Ourselves by Dr. David Stoop and Dr. James Masteller (c) 1991 by Dr. David Stoop. Published by Servant Publications, Box 8617, Ann Arbor, Michigan 48107. Used with permission. Based on work done by David H. Olsen, reported in David H. Olsen, Hamilton I. McCubbin and Associates, Families: What Makes Them Work, (Newbury Park, CA: Sage Publishing, 1989).

For each of the following statements, write in a number according to the following scheme for your family:

    1 — almost never true

    2 — sometimes true

    3 — almost always true

_____ 1.	Family members supported each other when they had problems
_____ 2.	Family members felt free to speak their minds
_____ 3.	It was easy to talk about almost anything with my family
_____ 4.	All family members participated in making family decisions
_____ 5.	Our family did many things together
_____ 6.	In our family, children had a say in how they were disciplined
_____ 7.	Our family loved to be in the same room together
_____ 8.	Our family enjoyed discussing problems and solutions
_____ 9.	Each of us knew that our friends were also family friends
_____ 10.	Everyone shared responsibilities in our family
_____ 11.	Family members shared interests with one another
_____ 12.	Rules changed often in our family

Now add up the totals for the odd and then the even statements and place them below.

Totals: _____ Even-numbered statements

_____ Odd-numbered statements

Place the even-numbered total on the Adaptability scale and the odd-numbered total on the Attachment scale.

ADAPTABILITY SCALE

Chaotic				Adaptable				Rigid			
6	7	8	9	10	11	12	13	14	15	16	17	18

ATTACHMENT SCALE

Disengaged				Attached				Enmeshed			
6	7	8	9	10	11	12	13	14	15	16	17	18

Adaptability—chaotic and rigid families have poor problem-solving capacities ingrained in their members, as well as having a hard time dealing with emotions.

- **Rigid**: Authoritarian, rules clear and non-negotiable
- **Chaotic**: No leadership, unknown arbitrary rules, decisions made in crises neither planned nor well thought out
- **Adaptable**: Clear but flexible leadership and healthy but adjustable discipline. Problems are discussed and various members may input a decision

Attachment—disengaged and enmeshed, has difficulty building healthy marital relationships. Relationships are either too close, or too far. Personal and family boundary confusion is present.

- **Enmeshed**: No individuality desired or fostered, extreme sense of closeness. Independence is looked upon as disloyalty. Boundaries are nonexistent within the family, but members keep others outside the family
- **Disengaged**: Value independence, and relationships outside

the family. Little togetherness

- **Attached:** Sense of individuality without a loss of connectedness. Do things together, but each is able to be active outside the family as well. The mutual respect that allows freedom of activity without hidden agendas that trigger guilt is present

The closer each linear scale is to the middle, the healthier the family. Wherever you end up on the scales, do not be dismayed. The goal is information and bringing how your family is/was to light so you will be healed. Take what you have found to God and ask Him to heal that part of you. Then, continue asking and watch what He will do as you open and submit yourself to Him and His healing in you!

CHAPTER 3

SALVATION & LETTING GO OF CONTROL

SALVATION

Salvation is the act of being saved. When Jesus said, "I am the door. If anyone enters by Me, he will be saved..." (John 10:9), He was speaking immediately of being saved from the penalty of sin and ultimately from the power and presence of sin. The penalty for your sin is eternal separation from God, which He doesn't want you to choose. According to John 3:17, "God did not send His Son into the world to condemn the world, but that the world through Him might be saved." Jesus paid the price for your sins on the cross and it is only through Him that you will be saved.

In the Old Testament, only the chief priest was allowed into the Holy of Holies once a year to make atonement for the people before God. When Jesus died, the veil (a curtain that was about 60 feet high, 30 feet wide and about four inches thick) that covered the opening to the Holy of Holies supernaturally ripped, starting at the top, signifying that the way to God was open to all who believed in Jesus' shed blood for their sins. Jesus also said, in John 3:3, "Most assuredly, I say to you, unless one is born again, he cannot see the kingdom of God." It is when you accept Jesus' shed blood for your sins that He sends His Holy Spirit to live within you to guide and speak to you. In 2 Corinthians 6:16, God said, "...I will dwell in them and walk among them; And I will be their God, and they shall be My people" (NASB).

When you accept the above, you become a child of the Most High God and God, in the person of the Holy Spirit, comes to dwell in you to lead and guide. The Spirit is powerful and being "born again" by having Him come and dwell within, is not to be taken lightly. He is not to be used by you but seeks rather to use you in loving God and others, even your enemies. "He" is used here to describe the Holy Spirit, as He is the third person of the Trinity. The Trinity is God, the Father, God, the Son (Jesus Christ), and God, the Holy Spirit. Each person of the Trinity is God, but in different forms, though they are still one. God, the Father, reveals Himself to you by sending His son, Jesus (both divine and human), to die on the cross. He then sends the Holy Spirit to dwell in you, who sincerely believe and accept Jesus' death and resurrection as payment for your sins and submit to His Lordship. In other words, God, in the form of the Holy Spirit, comes to dwell with and in each of us who accepts Jesus' work on the cross.

FAITH

Faith is belief and trust in what God says. It is turning away from unbelief, "casting all your cares upon Him, for He cares for you" (1 Peter 5:7). Faith is not only an intellectual acceptance of the truth but also a positive recognition and conviction of the truth as stated by God's Word. Paul wrote in Romans 10:17, "Faith comes by hearing, and hearing by the Word of God."

Unbelief will grow if you are not reading or hearing the Word of God. With unbelief, there's no belief or recognition that God is interested in every minute detail of your life. You may forget your privileged place before Him as His child and may struggle. You may stop believing that the Holy Spirit is interested in directing, guiding, talking, and truly touching you. You might feel alone. Well, why should you believe it? No one else was there for you as you were growing up! You might think, "Why should God be there?" The answer is because He is, always was, and always will be the personal God that He is and who loves you.

What is your view of God? How limited is it? Do you limit the Creator of the heavens and the earth? Yes, you likely do, as we all do. Your belief and view of God and the limits that you place on Him affect your response to Him and His Word.

What is your worldview? Do you believe and LIVE the belief that God made the earth and all that is in it? He has a plan for the world and for you as expressed in His Word? Do you live the belief that Jesus won victory on the cross over sin and death? For you?

It is one thing to confess belief and another to live it. As you become aware of any unbelief you may have, confess it to God and others and ask God to remove and heal that area in your life. That way, you can live your profession of faith honestly before God. In other words, it's OK to have unbelief but it's not OK to stay with it. Therefore, don't be afraid of any unbelief but acknowledge it and bring it to light so the Holy Spirit can work in and with you regarding your unbelief.

Your journey is one of learning to trust God, yourself, and others, with you. This is a sacred trust, considering that you and we are all "fearfully and wonderfully made" (Psalm 139:13). How precious are you, His creation! Do you recognize and wholeheartedly believe this? Though people in your past and present have likely harmed you, thus creating the potential for a skewed view of God and others, God wants you to know that He created you, knows you, and is with you, even if you do not feel His presence. "We walk by faith, not by sight," says God's Word (2 Corinthians 5:7). Know for sure that God is looking out for your best. He is waiting for you to sit, hear and listen to what He has to say to and for you. Your personal healing and faith will abound as you begin to recognize how much God loves you.

CONTROL

Control is trying to work things out on your own. It's a type of control that doesn't allow you to be who you were created to be. It is a fallacy to believe that if you control things, you will get what you want and will be happy. When you control yourself or others, no one is free to be who God made you and them to be.

Controlling is an attempt to gain something for yourself or to protect yourself and there are two issues here:

- The other person is not allowed to freely choose to give you what you want. You might attempt to manipulate them and play games with them. Whatever you will obtain won't satisfy because deep down, you know what you received was not freely given, thus not worthwhile or true

- Controlling protects yourself from your emotions and what you truly feel. You may not trust yourself to honor your opinions or emotions, so you put control around yourself as a protective measure. This lack of trust in Jesus Christ and in yourself is a faithless and ineffective way of dealing with the fear of the unknown

Control and manipulation are the opposite of faith, which is letting go and turning your life over to God and surrendering to the Holy Spirit. Submitting yourself to the Holy Spirit means not trying to control or manipulate others or situations to go your way.

Letting go of control does not mean you are a doormat and have no responsibility for your present or future. Quite the opposite. With letting go of control, true acceptance of the responsibility for yourself and your actions happens. As you do this, you begin to let go of the should, should nots, ought nots, have to and need to that you have been living by. How can letting go begin?

It begins by accepting responsibility for your behavior, which is difficult. It's so difficult you may live in denial, believing that you are good or that everything is fine. That only serves to bind you in discouragement, despair, and fear because you are not being truthful or honest. As you let go and hold out your hand in faith, you will move into the light where denial can be broken. You let go of control and the shutters begin to open. You begin to see your distorted perceptions of reality that have fostered destructive behaviors and you can begin admitting your responsibility for them. You begin to truly recognize that you are a sinner and even while this recognition happens, you begin to realize that you are loved and accepted, regardless of what you have done or will ever do.

In letting go of control, you decide to stop fighting the reality of who you are which is a waste of time. You get to accept yourself as Jesus Christ accepts you; just as you are. This does not mean you will stay that way, but it is the place to start. With this acceptance and surrender, you let your walls down and unflinchingly realize how human and imperfect you are. You begin to live in the truth about yourself and begin looking with understanding and compassion on yourself—something that's not easy to do! You become teachable and willing to listen to others. Communication begins to flourish, and you begin to feel connected. As this love and acceptance of yourself increases, you can, in turn, understand and love others. After all, the second greatest commandment is to love your neighbor as yourself.

This chapter is asking you to make a commitment to lay down your own will and life to God the Father, God the Son, and God, the Holy Spirit. There is acknowledgment of His Lordship and submission to it. It is decision time. Know that God is Lord, whether you decide to accept this truth or not.

The first chapter covered the covenantal God who loves you, and in the second chapter, that you are not all-powerful. There is one who is more holy and powerful than you are, and He is a person, Jesus Christ. Now, you can act on that knowledge by submitting yourself to His Lordship and be born again and renewed. Jesus said to Nicodemus, in John 3:3, "Most assuredly, I say to you, unless one is born again, he cannot see the kingdom of God." This is saying goodbye to the old and welcoming the new.

If you have not yet asked Jesus to forgive your sins and come into your life but are sincere about asking Him in, pray the following out loud to be born again spiritually, into God's kingdom:

Jesus, I am a sinner. I accept your sacrifice on the cross for my sins. I ask that You forgive me of my sins and come, dwell in my heart forever. I ask you to be my Lord and Savior. I know you died and rose again for me so that I may have eternal life (Romans 10:9-10). I recognize that by receiving Your forgiveness, this does not give me liberty to go out to continue sinning or doing wrong. I want to learn of and follow Your ways. Jesus, come into my life and mold and shape me to be who I have been created to be. I welcome the Holy Spirit and ask that He teach me Your ways. Amen.

Congratulations! If you have asked Jesus to be your Lord and Savior and come into your heart, you are now a child of God. Welcome to the family of God! You now have His Holy Spirit living within you as a seal that you are God's and are now part of His family! The Holy Spirit is also with you to be your counselor, give you wisdom, direct your path, and more. Below are some scriptures to think about and memorize to support the beginning of your new way of life.

> **John 15:5** *"I am the vine; you are the branches. He who abides in Me, and I in him, bears much fruit; for without Me, you can do nothing."*
>
> **Matthew 16:24-25** *"If anyone desires to come after Me, let him deny himself, and take up his cross, and follow Me. For anyone who wants to save his life will lose it, but anyone who loses his life for My sake will find it."*
>
> **Matt 6:25-34** *"Do not worry about your life, what you will eat or what you will drink...for tomorrow will worry about its own things. Sufficient for the day is its own trouble."*
>
> **Ephesians 1:17** *"May [God] give to you the spirit of wisdom and revelation in the knowledge of Him."*

Describe turning your will over to Jesus:

How do you think Jesus sees you, your life, and your problems? What do you feel He is thinking about you?

What doubts do you have that God can change you and your life for the better?

What fear do you have in trusting God with EVERY detail of your life?

A Way Of Life

How will giving your life over to God help to lessen the stress in your life?

How do you expect the Lord to help your path become straight?

What areas are you unwilling to turn over to God?

What does God say to you about worry, in Matt 6:25-34? *"Do not worry about your life, what you will eat or what you will drink...for tomorrow will worry about its own things. Sufficient for the day is its own trouble."*

What are you willing to do to remove worry from your life?

LETTING GO

The Bible is a book about relationships and responsibilities and the following statements express our responsibility to people we have relationships with. As we seek to understand how this works, God will teach us.

- To let go doesn't mean to stop caring; it means I cannot do certain things for others
- To let go is not to cut myself off; it's the realization that I cannot control others

- To let go is not always to shield, but to allow learning from natural consequences
- To let go is to admit powerlessness, which means the outcome is not in MY hands
- To let go is not to try to change or blame others; I can only change myself
- To let go is not to care for, but to care about
- To let go is not to judge, but to allow others to be human
- To let go is not to be in the middle arranging all the outcomes, but to allow others to affect their own outcomes
- To let go is not to deny, but to accept
- To let go is not to be overly protective, but to allow others and ourselves to face reality
- To let go is not to nag, scold, or argue, but to search out my own shortcomings and correct them
- To let go is not to adjust everything to my desires, but to take each day as it comes and cherish the moment
- To let go is not to criticize and regulate others, but to try to become what God means ME to be
- To let go is not to regret the past, but to grow and live for the future
- To let go is to fear less, hang on, and trust in Christ more; freely giving the love He has given to me

Author unknown

Who or what do you need to let go of: a rebellious child, a sorrow, a lost loved one, or a heartache you cannot change? Read this over, study it, pray over it, and you will find that letting go of your burden to God will release His peace to you.

In relationships, I see myself trying to manipulate in the following ways:

In relationships, blaming often plays a big part in the communication process, which hinders intimacy. Instead of a "win/win" situation, there is usually an "I won/you lost," or "you won/I lost scenario," which hurts intimacy.

My communications are usually: (Circle the one that applies)

- Me winning (I won/you lost)
- You winning (you won/I lost)
- Us winning (win/win)

I see myself blaming others most of the time for:

A Way Of Life

I blame myself for:

God asks that you work with others where they are and love them unconditionally. That does not mean that you do not address issues in a relationship. Look at THE WAY IT IS MEANT TO BE in the appendix to answer the following questions.

What is stated about your purpose for living?

What is stated about loving others without controlling them?

What does losing yourself to others mean?

I can best not lose myself to others by:

Why must a relationship be established by choice and not guilt or manipulation?

CHAPTER 4

SANCTIFICATION: PERSONAL GROWTH PLAN FOR ASSIMILATION & PRINCIPLE PRACTICE

Sanctification, according to Merriam-Webster, is defined as "the state of growing in divine grace as a result of Christian commitment after baptism or conversion." It is growing in grace and the emphasis is on the word, growing. This is not a stagnant walk, nor is it boring! But it is worth it. 😊 This principle will be covered in more detail in book 2 but for now, let's look at applying the principles just reviewed.

I call a certain time in my life, baptism by fire. I was living in a marriage with my unfaithful husband and believed that God could change my marriage (which I do believe is the truth—if BOTH parties are willing). So, I stayed in the marriage, hoping my husband would change his heart and mind. I knew that I was responsible for my part in the marriage, so began to pray that God would show me whatever I was doing wrong and change me. I asked God to create a clean heart in me and change my heart attitudes, motives and behaviors.

I went to God daily and asked Him to have His Holy Spirit search me. He began to show me gently, what needed to be changed, and as a gentleman, heal and clean my heart and teach me His ways. As I read the bible, I began to see how relationships and God's universal principles work and I became grateful and thankful for what He was showing me.

For the sanctification process to be effective, be sincere and willing to become aware of what doesn't line up with God's ways through reading His word. Ask Him to change what He shows you and do not resist the change by allowing Him to change you from the inside out. Do whatever action He says to do and don't worry or be scared, even if what you are learning is painful to admit or you don't completely understand, yet. God is a gentleman, and He will only work with you to the point that you allow Him to. Do you want to be fully healed? Free from all your fears? Don't resist and seek the Lord. He will be with you 100% of the way. As you let go of resistance, you will gain as the following depicts:

"No pain, No gain."

These are the words the athletes sing
As they work their muscles to the sting.

"It hurts, it hurts," they cry
As the burning goes deeper and deeper into their thigh.

And yet they push on to never-ending fights,
Knowing that without this pain, they would never reach the heights.

And so, I say to you — you who so resist your pain —
Work it to the bone and do not deter,
For with your pain, you will gain.

—WHAT WE RESIST, PERSISTS—

Plan

The intent of this book is for you to understand and apply the information and principles covered, which is imperative for living victoriously. Below is a growth and development plan for you to utilize with the goal of solidifying these life-giving principles in your life and all the lives that this work touches.

To create a personal growth development plan, start by defining what you've learned and what you want your results to be. Make sure you write them down. Next, perform a self-assessment and identify one area that needs attention. Then, determine the required actions and develop an action plan using the **SMARTER goal-setting method, found in the appendix.**

Here is an example of a growth plan.

What I want: To be effective as a leader of my family or at work.

What I do now:	What I learned:	What I will change:	The time period to practice my change:	The outcome:
I tend to control others and situations. I don't listen and make collaborative decisions with others.	I learned that surrendering frees me to be me. and that I don't have control over others. I only can control myself.	Listen with my heart before I speak. Listen for the truth and work with it only.	By the end of the next month.	1. My coworkers and family will notice and say something. 2. I will feel open on the inside rather than stressed and closed off.

Implement with goals: (see appendix on how to set goals)

Example of a SMARTER goal with its supporting activities to reach the stated goal. The scale used is from 1-10 with 10 being high.

Goal: By the end of next month, my family and coworkers will see me as an effective leader, as evidenced by them saying something about my behavior change, and my stress score will reduce from an 8 to a 4.

Simple:	yes
Measurable:	stress score lower, family/coworkers say something about my behavior change
Achievable:	this is achievable
Realistic:	this is realistic
Timely:	end of the next month
Evaluate goal:	end of next month and stress level reduction
Reset goal:	change it, extend the end time, or create another goal

Activities:

1. For the next month, at work and in every meeting, I will not be the first to speak and share my opinion. I will share...just not first!
2. For the next month, I will listen with my heart to what my family says and seek to understand their perspective before stating mine. I will do that by asking questions.

Nancy Williams

Now, it's your turn!

On a separate piece of paper that you can hang where you will see it frequently, type or write out your growth plan to assimilate and apply the principles you just learned. Find a safe friend who will listen and share your plan with them, and as someone I know says, "git'r done!"

CONCLUSION

As A Way of Life, in its full workbook format, was so meaty, I was advised to divide the work into multiple small courses. Therefore, I have divided A Way of Life, Kingdom Principles for Living Victoriously, into 4 parts and this concludes Book 1. There is much more that leads to peace within and I want to encourage you to continue learning and applying God's principles so that you *will* experience freedom and peace within.

To continue your journey & in your internet browser, type in AWayofLifeMinistries.com. Click on the Store or Courses tab to find resources and purchase whatever you need to continue your journey and growth. You can also search on Amazon for A Way of Life by Nancy Williams to purchase from there.

Please let us know how your journey is going by using the Contact Us form on the website to connect with us. We would LOVE to hear from you about how you are progressing. You can also subscribe to our blog page and we'll keep you informed of upcoming events, new publications, online courses, and book offerings. Hope to hear from you soon, and if you have questions, please ask!

Blessings on your journey

~ Nancy ~

SUGGESTED READING LIST

The following 4 books are secular but may be helpful. Read them with caution and a biblically discerning mind.

- Beattie, Melody. (1987). Codependent No More. New York: Harper & Row.
- Bradshaw, John. (1988). The Family. Florida: Health Communications, Inc.
- Fromm, Erich. (1956). The Art of Loving. New York: Harper & Row.
- Peck, M. Scott, MD. (1978). The Road Less Traveled. NY: Simon & Schuster, Inc.

The following list is from a Christian perspective. I encourage you to read especially Francis Schaeffer's, True Spirituality, R.A. Torry's, The Person and Work of the Holy Spirit, and J. Keith Miller's, A Hunger for Healing.

- Bennett, Dennis and Rita. (1971). The Holy Spirit and You. New Jersey: Logos Int.
- Bridges, Jerry. (1978). The Pursuit of Holiness. Colorado: Navpress.
- Bridges, Jerry. (1983). The Practice of Godliness. Colorado: Navpress.
- Buhler, Rich. (1988). Pain and Pretending. Tennessee: Thomas Nelson, Inc.
- Esses, Michael. (1974). The Phenomenon of Obedience. New

Jersey: Logos Int.

- Huggett, Joyce. (1986). The Joy of Listening to God. Illinois: InterVarsity Press.
- Miller, J. Keith. (1991). A Hunger for Healing. New York: Harper Collins.
- Powell, John. (1969). Why Am I Afraid to Tell You Who I Am?. Illinois: Argus Comm.
- Powell, John. (1974). The Secret of Staying in Love. Texas: Argus Communications.
- Powell, John. (1976). Fully Human, Fully Alive. Illinois: Argus Communications.
- Powell, John. (1978). Unconditional Love. Texas: Argus Communications.
- Schaeffer, Francis A. (1971). True Spirituality. Illinois: Tyndale House Publishers.
- Seamands, David A. (1981). Healing for Damaged Emotions. Illinois: SP Pub., Inc.
- Smalley, Gary and Trent, John, Ph.D. (1986), The Blessing. Tennessee: Thomas Nelson, Inc.
- Smith, Chuck. (1979,1980). Effective Prayer Life. California: The Word For Today.
- Swindoll, Charles R. (1983). Dropping Your Guard. New York: Bantam Books.
- Torrey, R.A. (1974). The Person & Work of the Holy Spirit (rev. ed.). Michigan: Zondervan Publishing House.
- Watson, David. (1980). The Hidden Battle. Illinois: Harold Shaw Publishers.

- Whitfield, Charles L., M.D. (1987). Healing the Child Within. Florida: Health Communications, Inc.

- Wilkerson, David; and Sherrill, John & Elizabeth. (1963). The Cross and The Switchblade. New Jersey: Spire Books

APPENDIX TABLE OF CONTENTS

It is recommended to review and use all the resources in this appendix to continue your growth journey and find your blessings as you do so.

USING A WAY OF LIFE IN A GROUP SETTING 68

DEPENDENCE ON GOD 70

DAILY ACCEPTANCE PRAYER 72

THE FIRST AND SECOND GREATEST COMMANDMENTS 73

THE TEN COMMANDMENTS 75

THE WAY IT IS MEANT TO BE 77

GOAL SETTING 79

BIBLIOGRAPHY 85

ABOUT THE AUTHOR 90

USING A WAY OF LIFE IN A GROUP SETTING

This book has been used in multiple group settings, so the below has been included to support group success and encourage individuals to be facilitators. Usually, there is a sharing of what God is doing in each person and what spoke to them from the chapter being reviewed.

GROUP LEADERS

Ground Rules, which are to be read to the small group:

- Confidentiality is of utmost importance
- Please don't put down another's person, thoughts, or opinions—each person is of equal value
- It's OK to say that you don't want to share
- Please share time equally. Give everyone a chance to share
- One person talks at a time
- Please be personal. Use "I" or "me" statements
- We work together as a team
- Talk from feelings, not stories or circumstances
- Don't give advice
- Listen and try to understand what is being said

Good Family Functional Rules are taken from: The Family by John Bradshaw. Copyright 1988. Health Communications, Inc. Used with permission from the author and if used in the group, the group will be healthy. Facilitators are to read the following Functional Rules at the beginning of each group.

A Way Of Life

- Problems are acknowledged and resolved

  5 freedoms—can be expressed and explored with no judgment:
  - ✓ Perceptions
  - ✓ Feelings
  - ✓ Thoughts
  - ✓ Desires
  - ✓ Fantasies
- Communication is direct, specific, and behavioral
- Family members get their needs met
- Family members can be different
- Parents do what they say (self-disciplined disciplinarians)
- Atmosphere is fun and spontaneous
- The rules require accountability
- Violation of another's values leads to guilt
- Mistakes are forgiven and viewed as learning tools
- Individuals are in touch with their healthy shame
- The family systems exist for each other

What to discuss in the group setting:

- What was particularly meaningful to you from the last chapter?
- How do you see this affecting your life right now?
- Are there any changes that you want to make?

Closing in Prayer: What can we pray about tonight or this next week?

DEPENDENCE ON GOD

See below, where God is in the middle, and all the spokes have their focus on Him and His way. Walk through steps 1-11 in order and watch the results within yourself! The result is having the change desired.

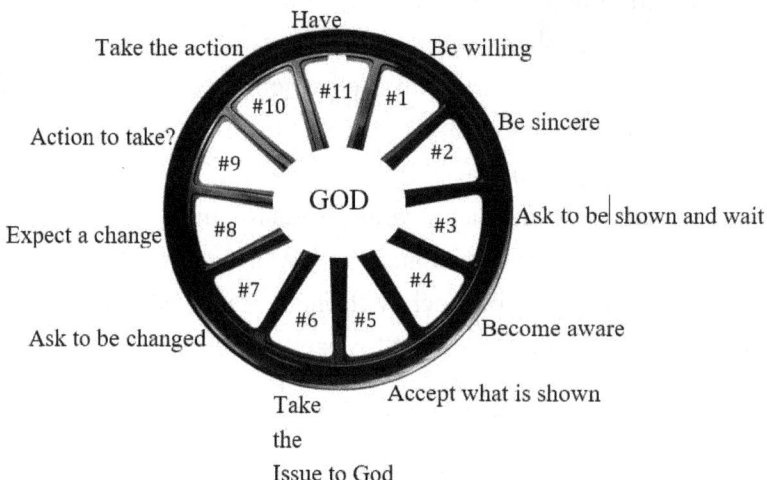

The beginning of your dependence on God starts with your being willing, and goes until you BE, DO, and then Have, regarding each particular situation. Be willing & sincere, ask to be shown, and God will open your heart and you will begin to be aware of what you get to know. Accepting this knowledge is critical to your personal & spiritual growth. Take what God shows you back to Him and ask for it and for you to be changed. Expect Him to work within you and you will know when things are changing. He may show you some action to take, so make sure you complete the action and you will be closer to being or having what He wants you to be or have.

A Way Of Life

This cycle works for everything and while most elements are important, being willing and sincere to ask to be shown what needs to be changed, or ask for understanding, etc. is most important. If you are not sincere or willing, this cycle of growth and understanding will not work.

Point # 1	You are WILLING
Point # 2	You are SINCERE
Point # 3	You ASK TO BE SHOWN
Point # 4	You are AWARE
Point # 5	You ACCEPT WHAT WE ARE SHOWN
Point # 6	You TAKE THE ISSUE TO GOD
Point # 7	You ASK TO BE CHANGED
Point # 8	You EXPECT A CHANGE
Point # 9	You look for what ACTION TO TAKE
Point # 10	You TAKE THE ACTION
Point # 11	You BE, DO, then HAVE

To refresh the understanding of what is meant by the BE—DO—HAVE statement, refer to the introduction at the beginning of this book. Then, enjoy and experience the newfound freedom which God gives to you as you submit and depend on Him!

DAILY ACCEPTANCE PRAYER

Retype or print this for yourself. Acceptance does not mean that you are a victim or doormat. Acceptance supports clear thinking and a clear heart to hear the truth.

Acceptance is the answer to all my problems today—

When I'm disturbed, it is because I feel some person, place, thing, or situation is unacceptable to me.

I can find no serenity until I accept that person, place, thing, or situation as being exactly the way it is supposed to be at this moment.

Nothing happens in God's world by mistake.

Until I accept responsibility for my attitudes, I cannot have peace in my life.

Unless I accept life completely on life's terms, I cannot be happy.

I get to concentrate not so much on what gets to be changed in the world around me as on what gets to be changed in my attitudes and in me.

Thank You, Lord, for the day You have made.

Author unknown

THE FIRST AND SECOND GREATEST COMMANDMENTS

Loving One Another As Ourselves

In Matthew 22:36-40 we find a great answer to a truly great question. The question is, "Which is the greatest commandment in the law?" Jesus' profound answer is "'You shall love the Lord your God with all your heart...soul, and...mind.' This is the first and greatest commandment. And the second is like it: 'You shall love your neighbor as yourself.' On these two commandments hang all the Law and the Prophets."

What is this love all about? First, we receive God's mercy (not condemning judgment) for ourselves and then extend it to others. As we evaluate ourselves honestly before God, we begin to see our sinfulness. Acknowledging and repenting of our sinfulness before God and receiving His forgiveness through Christ puts us in a right relationship with Him. He then begins to change us. As we see how sinful we are before the Holy One and receive His mercy (no condemnation with repentance), we can better understand and love others while extending to them the mercy we received (the love really extends from God).

Loving one another also includes chastising and correcting one another. As God's Holy Spirit convicts us and holds us accountable to Him, so we are to be accountable to others and receive their correction as well as correct them. That does not give us the liberty to open our mouths and speak without loving discernment. Rather, this is a heavy responsibility to act in love and not condemnation towards others—to hate the sin but love the sinner. Personal attacks are not allowed in God's family, which grows together in all the frailties of our human nature. As we live together as a family, we become aware of each other's shortcomings. As that happens, first pray: Pray for the person, and ask God if He desires you to speak to the other person. Be careful and let wisdom and caution be your guide since damage is easily done to others but not easily repaired. If in doubt, ask a mature, trusted Christian for godly guidance.

THE TEN COMMANDMENTS

The following are the Ten Commandments given by God in Exodus 20 and repeated in Deuteronomy 5. Many individuals have never read these, though they have heard of them. Echoing the two greatest commandments summarized by Jesus, notice that the first four commandments teach us how to love God, and the last six, how to love others.

Commandment 1:

"I am the Lord your God... You shall have no other gods before Me."

Worship only our creator, who is one God, yet three distinct Persons: God the Father, God the Son, and God the Holy Spirit.

Commandment 2:

"You shall not make for yourself a carved image. You shall not bow down to them, nor serve them. For I, the Lord your God, am a jealous God."

Do not worship things. Worship God alone.

Commandment 3:

"You shall not take the name of the Lord your God in vain."

Never use God's name as a swear word or make fun of holy things.

Commandment 4:

"Remember the Sabbath day; to keep it holy."

Keep God's Day special and use it for Him.

Commandment 5:

"Honor your father and your mother, that your days may be long, and that it may be well with you."

Love and obey your parents.

Commandment 6:

"You shall not murder."

Because man is made in God's image, never take a life unless absolutely necessary.

Commandment 7:

"You shall not commit adultery."

Do not take another person's husband or wife.

Commandment 8:

"You shall not steal."

Respect the property of others.

Commandment 9:

"You shall not bear false witness against your neighbor."

Do not lie about anyone.

Commandment 10:

"You shall not covet your neighbor's wife; and you shall not desire your neighbor's house, his field, or anything that is your neighbor's." (no heart attitude of coveting)

THE WAY IT IS MEANT TO BE

Free from worry,
Free from fear,
Trusting You.

-THIS IS THE WAY-

Separate to You alone,
Living out what God ordained for me,
For why else should I be here?

-THIS IS THE WAY-

Sharing myself with others but
Not losing myself to them in the process,
For I belong to You alone.

-THIS IS THE WAY-

Receiving from others,
Loving them deeply with all my being, but
Knowing that they belong to You alone.

-THIS IS THE WAY-

Free to fly to the music of Your joy,
Free to enjoy Your earth with thanks and praises,
Free to feel Your wind blowing through my hair,
Free to feel Your waves tumble me in playfulness,

Free to experience others in separateness.
FREE CHOICE

-THE WAY IT IS MEANT TO BE-

Nancy Williams

GOAL SETTING

Many individuals have never been taught about goal setting. This exercise will teach you how to clearly state your goals and then set up subgoals (activities) to achieve them.

First—why should you set goals? Isn't God supposed to do everything for you? He can intervene and move you where He wants you to be, can't He? So, why do you have to do anything?

Yes, God can move you if He so desires to work that way. Most often, He doesn't. He can speak to you, but it is up to you to act as His vessel here on earth. Setting goals can be for any part of your life—for what God has spoken to your heart for you to do, for your own growth, education, or fun.

When goals are set, there's something that will arise in you to begin working to complete the goal. A purpose will grow within you and skimming along in life doing who knows what ends. Goals don't have to be great feats, but as you begin setting goals and moving forward, God directs your path. You can direct a moving car, but not a parked car. Goals help you get moving!

Think of the term SMARTER to support you in writing your goals:

    Specific (make it simple and clear)

    Measurable

    Achievable

    Realistic

    Timely

Evaluate

Reset goal

Sample Goal:

I will study my Bible 4 times a week for 1 hour over a one-month period.

S:	personal Bible study
M:	4 times/week
A:	clearly stated
R:	can be achieved
T:	over a month's time (specify which month)
E:	to be done after a month's time or throughout the month
R:	select another month or pick different Bible-study goals

Subgoals (or activities) are those behaviors or specific activities you must do to achieve your expected end. In the example above, some activities might include:

- setting the alarm earlier
- choose the place and time for Bible study
- not planning anything else for that time frame
- turning phones and TVs off

You can be as creative as you want to be.

On the following pages, write down goals that you want to incorporate in your life and the sub-goals or activities needed to achieve them, using the SMARTER way of setting goals.

A Way Of Life

LIFE DOMAIN GOALS

Life Domains (adjust the following to your needs)

Spiritual goals: **Activities**

Health and fitness: **Activities**

Job: **Activities**

Education: Activities

Social/Family: Activities

Recreation: Activities

Financial: **Activities**

List an area of your life and write down where you see God leading you in that area within the next year, 5 years, and 10 years. You can repeat this with any area of your life. If you do not have any direction right now, seek the Lord and begin to make plans but be ever watchful in case you are going off His path for you. He will let you know and guide you as you move out. Proverbs 16:9 states, "A man's heart plans his way, but the Lord directs his steps." Proverb 16:3 promises, that when you "commit your works to the Lord, your thoughts will be established." How wonderful to know that He will give you clear and solid thoughts as you trust and obey Him!

Area:

1 year:

Nancy Williams

5 years:

10 years:

BIBLIOGRAPHY

Andrews, Andy. (2002). The Traveler's Gift. Tennessee: Thomas Nelson, Inc.

Beattie, Melody. (1987). Codependent No More. New York: Harper & Row.

Bender, Stephanie & Keleher, Kathleen. (1991). PMS—A Positive Program to Gain Control. New York: The Body Press.

Bennett, Dennis & Rita. (1971). The Holy Spirit and You. New Jersey: Logos International.

Berkhof, Louis. (1933). Manual of Christian Doctrine. Michigan: William B. Eerdmans Publishing Company.

Bradshaw, John. (1988). The Family. Florida: Health Communications, Inc.

Bridges, Jerry. (1978). The Pursuit of Holiness. Colorado: Navpress.

Bridges, Jerry. (1983). The Practice of Godliness. Colorado: Navpress.

Buhler, Rich. (1988). Pain and Pretending. Tennessee: Thomas Nelson, Inc.

Burkett, Larry. (1990). The Financial Planning Workbook. Chicago: Moody Press.

Campbell, Roderick. (1954). Israel and the New Covenant. Pennsylvania: Presbyterian and Reformed Publishing Company.

Cloud, H., & Townsend, J. (1992). Boundaries. Michigan: Zondervan

Publishing House.

Corey, Gerald F. (1977). Theory and Practice of Counseling and Psychotherapy (2nd ed.). California: Wadsworth.

Dileo, Sandy. (1984). "Stress Management". California: Author.

Edman, V. Raymond. (1948). The Disciplines of Life. Minnesota: World Wide Publications.

Elwell, Walter A. (Editor). (1989). Evangelical Commentary on the Bible. Michigan: Baker Book House.

Engstrom, Ted W. (1976). The Making of a Christian Leader. Michigan: Zondervan Publishing House.

Erickson, Millard J. (1985). Christian Theology. Michigan: Baker Book House.

Esses, Michael. (1974). The Phenomenon of Obedience. New Jersey: Logos International.

Felber, Terry. (2002), Am I Making Myself Clear? Nashville: Thomas Nelson.

Foster, Richard. (1992). Prayer—Finding the Heart's True Home. California: Harper.

Fromm, Erich. (1956). The Art of Loving. New York: Harper & Row.

Green, Michael. (1975). I Believe in the Holy Spirit. Michigan: Wm. B. Eerdmans Publishing Company.

Hammond, Frank & Ida. (1973). Pigs In the Parlor. Missouri: Impact Books.

Hart, S.L. (1968). Lifetime of Love. Mass: Daughters of St. Paul.

Johnson, Spencer, MD. (1998). Who Moved My Cheese? USA: Penguin Group.

Lancaster, Wade & Jeanette. (1982). "Rational Decision Making: Managing Uncertainty." Journal of Nursing Administration. Sept. 1982. pgs. 23-28.

Leman, Dr. Kevin. (1981). Sex Begins in the Kitchen. California: Regal Books.

MacNutt, Francis, O.P. (1974). Healing. Indiana: Ave Maria Press.

Martin, Dr. Walter. (1962). Essential Christianity. California: GL Publications.

Martin, Francis P. (1979). Hung by the Tongue. Louisiana: F.P.M. Publications.

Maxwell, John C. (2023). The 16 Undeniable Laws of Communication. Maxwell Leadership Publishing

McAll, Dr. Kenneth. (1982). Healing the Family Tree. Great Britain: Sheldon Press.

Moody, Dwight L. (1881). Secret Power. California: Regal Books.

Murphy, Dr. Ed. (1992). The Handbook for Spiritual Warfare. Tennessee: Thomas Nelson Publishers, Inc.

Nutrition Search, Inc. (1973). Nutrition Almanac. New York: McGraw-Hill Book Company.

Payne, Leanne. (1991). Restoring the Christian Soul Through Healing Prayer. Illinois: Crossway Books.

Peck, M. Scott, MD. (1978). The Road Less Traveled. New York: Simon & Schuster, Inc.

Peck, M. Scott, MD. (1983). People of the Lie. New York: Simon & Schuster, Inc.

Penner, Clifford & Joyce. (1981). The Gift of Sex. Texas: Word, Inc.

Powell, John. (1969). Why Am I Afraid to Tell You Who I Am?.

Illinois: Argus Communications.

Powell, John. (1974). The Secret of Staying in Love. Texas: Argus Communications.

Powell, John. (1976). Fully Human, Fully Alive. Illinois: Argus Communications.

Powell, John. (1978). Unconditional Love. Texas: Argus Communications.

Ross, Elisabeth Kübler-. (1960). On Death & Dying. Simon & Schuster/Touchstone.

Sanders, J. Oswald. (1967). Spiritual Leadership. Illinois: Moody Bible Institute.

Schaeffer, Francis A. (1971). True Spirituality. Illinois: Tyndale House Publishers.

Seamands, David A. (1981). Healing for Damaged Emotions. Illinois: SP Publications, Inc.

Smalley, Gary & Trent, John, Ph.D. (1986). The Blessing. Tennessee: Thomas Nelson, Inc.

Smalley, Gary & Trent, John, Ph.D. (1988). The Language of Love. California: Focus on the Family.

Smalley, Gary & Trent, John, Ph.D. (1990). The Two Sides of Love. Colorado: Focus on the Family.

Smith, Chuck. (1980). Effective Prayer Life. California: The Word for Today.

Swindoll, Charles R. (1983). Dropping Your Guard. New York: Bantam Books.

Taylor, Richard Shelley. (1962). The Disciplined Life. Minnesota: Bethany House Publishers.

Torrey, R.A. (1974 revised edition). The Person & Work of the Holy Spirit. Michigan: Zondervan Publishing House.

Vine, W. E. (1981). Vine's Expository Dictionary of Old and New Testament Words. New Jersey: Fleming H. Revell Company.

Watson, David. (1980). The Hidden Battle. Illinois: Harold Shaw Publishers.

White, Tom. (1993). Breaking Strongholds: How Spiritual Warfare Sets Captives Free. Michigan: Servant Publications.

Whitfield, Charles L., M.D. (1987). Healing the Child Within. Florida: Health Communications, Inc.

Wilkerson, David & Sherrill, John & Elizabeth. (1963). The Cross and The Switchblade. New Jersey: Spire Books.

Wilkerson, David. (1972). The Pocket Promise Book. California: Regal Books.

Williams, Dr. Roger J. (1971). Nutrition Against Disease. New York: Pitman Publishing Corporation.

ABOUT THE AUTHOR

My heart's cry is one of freedom and abundance for you, who read this. I was born and raised in the Panama Canal Zone and accepted Jesus Christ as my Lord and Savior between the ages of 10-13. During my childhood, God called me off by myself to spend time with Him reading His Word, next to the sparkling blue Caribbean water. He was my teacher and even with that, many mistakes did I make! When I was 17, He called me to be a Registered Nurse and it was during one of my areas of work that an earlier edition of this book was born.

I married at 22 to an unbeliever, was divorced at 30, and went through what I call baptism by fire during my first marriage. God had me clean up all I was doing that was unloving nor supporting my marriage regardless of what my ex-husband was or was not doing. Doing what is right because it is right, is the right thing to do though it's not easy. Especially when my own needs were not being met! The earlier edition of this book was completed during this season of life, and I began teaching these kingdom principles of living a victorious life in the community for many years.

During the writing process, there were many times that I stopped as I did not know what the next step was. I sought the Lord, and He answered me through a sense of knowing, and only then did I move

A Way Of Life

on and continued this journey. One summer, I remember sitting at my desk while the sun was shining brightly on the deep-colored greenery outside my window. I looked at everyone playing while I sat working with the sun playing on the leaves. I chose to not get up and play because, above all else, my heart's cry is one of freedom and abundance for you who read this. Even then, I knew that to create something requires sacrifice and I knew that I would either get my reward later or maybe never. And the reward didn't even matter. What was and still is important, is that I finish the work I promised God I would and was called to do.

I have since remarried, have a wonderful family, and look forward to more of God's blessings in my life as I give to others! May you ask Him for your way and follow it. Therein is fulfillment and blessings galore. Why else are we to be here but to live out what was ordained for each of us from the beginning of time? That is why this work was written. That is why this work was written for you.

                With blessings always,

                Nancy Williams

www.ingramcontent.com/pod-product-compliance
Lightning Source LLC
Chambersburg PA
CBHW060357050426
42449CB00009B/1777